Renga Variations

For my son, Chris, with love

Sean Lause

Cyberwit.net
HIG 45 Kaushambi Kunj, Kalindipuram
Allahabad - 211011 (U.P.) India
http://www.cyberwit.net
Tel: +(91) 9415091004
E-mail: info@cyberwit.net

Printed at Repro India Limited.

Preface

These poems are not traditional Renga but variations designed to preserve the call-and-response structure of the original format within a looser, more open framework.

Renga, or "Linked Verse," originated in Japan during the Twelfth Century. It consists of one set of lines with a general structure of 5-7-5 syllables, followed by an answering set of 7-7 syllables. One poet would compose the 5-7-5 link, then another poet would respond with a 7-7 link, yet another with a new 5-7-5, and so on. It was a communal art form, binding word to word, line to line, stanza to stanza, poem to poem, poet to poet. It was a beautiful culture speaking to itself.

The supposed "5-7-5" syllable count is actually quite flexible in Japanese. A Japanese haiku translated literally into English would have closer to eleven or twelve syllables. Flexibility is also possible in the other direction if more syllables are needed. As Basho said, "Even if you have three or four extra syllables—or as many as five or seven—you need not worry as long as the verse sounds right." Basho here anticipates the "Sprung Rhythm" of Gerard Manley Hopkins. The challenge in Renga or Haiku is to use words to escape words, to share one's poetic experience with the reader through the power of the image, and what I love most about Renga is that the reader then becomes the writer and the writer the reader. The linked poem flows over the wall of the self into another, questioning the very concept of a central, isolate identity.

My love for Renga and Haiku stems from the power of Japanese poetry to overflow the syllable, the word, the line and the stanza, to make boundaries fluid and one image resonate with another, then another, and so forth, uniting poet and nature, writer and reader, self and other. R. H. Blyth wrote: "Every haiku…has a kind of fluidity…we see things in their manifold relations…" In a haiku, two separate images are juxtaposed to create this sense of sudden similarity, creating what J.

Hillis Miller calls "a resonance between the images themselves. Nothing exists in isolation." This ability to transcend the personal ego and "enter in" to nature or another person the haiku poets called "Shasei," or "entering in," a concept akin to Keats's "Negative Capability." The wall between self and other dissolves, proving to have been a mere illusion from the start. Basho wrote: "Only he who has arrived…does not take himself as separate from things, but identifies himself with them in their essential activity…Your poetry issues of its own accord, when you and the object have become one…Learn of the bamboo from the bamboo." Haiku, then, which appears on the surface to be a closed form with its 5-7-5 structure, is in fact also quite open, allowing the outside—nature, the object seen, the reader—into the poem itself.

Renga also appears on first glance to be a closed form (5-7-5/7-7), yet because it is a linked verse it is also open, and so long as there are enough writers and readers, may continue indefinitely, like the "All Over" look and feel of a painting by Jackson Pollock.

I first began writing haiku because of rejection. The first poems I wrote and sent to literary magazines were almost all rejected because they were too long. At that point in my life I was very influenced by Allen Ginsberg and John Ashbury. Clearly my long poems were not nearly as well-written as theirs! So I decided to pare my poems down, to simplify. I began to write and submit haiku. I had some success here, so one day I started writing haiku in clusters, then I would turn each cluster into a poem, each stanza essentially one haiku, yet the whole poem unified around a central image, set of images, or emotion.

This worked well enough for a while, but I wanted to bring more fluidity and openness into the poem so I could clearly link the haiku and make the poem more unified. To do this, I adopted four poetic techniques I borrowed from the Japanese:

1 The verse quote
2 Juxtaposition of images
3 The Renga stanza flow
4 Pivoting

The verse quote

Many haiku open with a line that echoes a haiku from another poet in a kind of "call-and-response." For example, here is a poem by the Twelfth Century poet, Saigyo:

> Little did I guess
> I'd ever pass so many years…
> or even this mountain again
> still alive,
> here on Mount Dead of Night

Saigyo's poetry deeply influenced Basho, who opens this haiku using the fourth line of Saigyo's poem:

> still alive
> under the slightness of my hat,
> enjoying the coolness.

As Jane Reichhold notes, "Like Saigyo before him, Basho believed in co-dependent origination, a Buddhist idea holding that all things are fully interdependent, even at the point of origin; that no thing can be completely self-originating."

Many of the poems in *Renga Variations* open with a quote from another author, and sometimes that line serves as the first line of my poem. I enjoy the sound and feel of one voice overflowing into another, both poems performing a kind of duet or dance down the page, rather than the focus we in the West tend to place on the isolate "I."

Juxtaposition of images

In haiku, nothing exists alone. Rather, life is defined by relation. The self depends on the not-self (sabi, emptiness), the one on the other. As the greatest of haiku scholars, R.H. Blyth wrote: "Every haiku…has Again, we see Blyth's "manifold relations" at work. So a haiku often places two images or events next to one another, without explanation or commentary. This gap, or silence, creates a resonance, an echo, a kind of electric charge between the juxtaposed images. The reader feels challenged or inspired to fill the gap, to close up a meaning, and so participates in the constructed meaning of the poem itself, bridging the space between writer and reader. And yet there is still the sense that this is only a construction, that somehow the mystery the poem has tapped into is still unsolved, and perhaps should not be solved, since the beauty of the poem and of the experience it expresses lie just within that mystery, that silence.

Here is an example from Basho:

The restless sea,
flowing toward Sado Isle,
the River of Heaven

"The River of Heaven" is the Milky Way. Without external commentary, the poem juxtaposes the restless sea with the calm of heaven, merging above and below.

One of my favorite haikus is this one from Issa:

Don't worry, spider,
I keep house
casually.

This poem juxtaposes civilization (the house) with nature (the spider). Both humans and arachnids need a home. Note here the gaps in the text that the poem invites the reader to complete. When I returned to this poem years after I had first read it, I was surprised to see that the poem makes no reference either to a web or a broom. I had imagined those two objects myself—one belonging to nature, one belonging to civilization—but both necessary for living creatures to maintain some coherent order in their lives. Issa had invited me inside his poem, and the resulting imagery was part his and part my own. If a stanza is a "little room," the haiku poet's room has a door in one wall.

The Renga stanza flow

The 5-7-5 haiku structure is still, nevertheless, a little room. However, the 5-7-5 stanza followed by a 7-7 stanza of Renga creates a call-and-response structure that allows ideas, emotions, and images to flow from one stanza to another and from one writer to another.

The pivot

Jane Reichhold defines this haiku technique thusly: "In the pivot…the middle line acts as a gate that can swing in either direction. This results from having a middle line that can have two meanings. The reader is flipped from one thing to another." As an example, Reichhold cites this poem by Basho:

First snowfall
almost finished
on the bridge

Reichhold notes: "Here both the snowfall and the work on the bridge were "almost finished"".

The pivot line overflows the little wall of silence that usually occurs at the end of one line of a poem. Moreover, it requires the reader to go back and re-read the line before the pivot line, then loop down to the line following the pivot line. As a result, the reader becomes an active participant in constructing the sound, feel, and meaning of the poem. Also, please note that, as with Issa, this poem also overlaps the visible with the invisible. Here it is the workers building the bridge who are invisible. Apparently their work began in the Fall; now they have some time off, but must know they need to return soon to finish their work as soon as possible. Yet it is precisely the unfinished nature of the bridge that Basho finds beautiful. Like the workers, he too is invisible, since he is not pictured in the poem though he is standing on the bridge himself, admiring it. It is the reader who must imagine him, just as he imagines the workers, and by doing so the reader is invited inside the poem. Any wall of consciousness between self and other, nature and civilization, poem and reader, has been transcended.

The haiku concept of the pivot is similar in some ways to Pierre Reverdy's method of overlapping his lines. For example, here is his poem, "Air":

Air

Something forgotten

               closed door

On the sloping earth
A tree trembles
      All alone
         A bird is singing
     On the roof
All the light left
      Is the sun
And the gestures your fingers make.

The first pivot line here is "All alone," which can apply both to "A tree trembles" and "A bird is singing." The lines might be written:

A tree trembles
all alone.
All alone
a bird is singing.

But the repetition of "all alone" would border on the sentimental. The loneness of things, to Reverdy, is not something to be pitied. Aloneness is just the way things are, their "thisness," what Basho would call "Sabi." Moreover, by using one line to do double-duty, Reverdy overflows one line into another, and one image into another, weaving his text into a unity. Another pivot line here is "On the roof." This could be written as:

A bird is singing
on the roof.
On the roof
all the light left
is the sun.

But this repetition would focus the reader's attention too much on that roof, which is, after all, only a roof. It is not the object per se that interests Reverdy, but rather *the relations between things*. Reverdy's world is a paradox, a world in which we all feel terribly alone while at the same time we are not alone at all. We are related to our language, which is deeply interwoven, where words flow and overlap, and no wall can stop this process. On one level, we are alone. At least we often feel alone, alien, isolate. Yet at the same time, everything in this world corresponds with its environment, what Wordsworth calls "things forever speaking." Reality is a relation.

Another poet who used the pivot method was Frank O'Hara. For example:

The warm walking night
wandering
amusement of darkness.

The night is wandering, as is the amusement within the night. Pivoting over-determines a word or phrase, creating a rich sense of echo and resonance. Words, objects, even people that might not appear on first glance to be related are woven into the text of the poem

A master of the pivot was Emily Dickinson, though there is no evidence that she knew about Renga. Literary historian Greg Mattingly calls this quality of Dickinson her "Double Duty Words," and calls this method "practically a Dickinson signature." For example, in her classic poem, "A Bird Came Down the Walk":

A Bird came down the Walk—
He did not know I saw—
He bit an Angleworm in halves
and ate the fellow, raw,

And then he drank a Dew
from a convenient Grass—
And then hopped sidewise to the Wall
to let a Beetle pass—

He glanced with rapid eyes
That hurried all around—
They looked like frightened Beads, I thought—
He stirred his Velvet head

Like one in danger, Cautious,
I offered him a crumb
And he unrolled his feathers
And rowed him softer home—

Than oars divide the Ocean,
Too silver for a seam—
Or Butterflies, off Banks of Noon
Leap, plashless as they swim.

If Dickinson had placed a period after "head," then the adjective "Cautious" would modify the speaker, and the speaker would be the one who feels in danger. But by placing a comma after this word instead, Dickinson over-determines this word, so that two readings are possible:

"He stirred his Velvet head
like one in hunger, Cautious."
And:

"Like one in danger, Cautious,
I offered him a crumb."

This doubling allows the speaker's spirit to overlap with its subject. Both bird and human share a sense of vulnerability, and are uncomfortable with being observed. In this moment of vision, the observer and the observed blend into one, and the separate self of the poet is briefly transcended. "This feature," Mattingly claims, "is found in many Dickinson poems, where a line or group of lines can be read as going with either of two different parts of the poem."

Like the Eastern poets, then, some Western poets also pivot and overlap their words and lines in order to create a more vibrant and multi-layered perception.

Subtext

However, my interest in poetry is not merely aesthetic, and like the poets of renga and haiku, I do not believe that a poem can be isolated from the world around it. The poems in *Renga Variations* also contain a subtext. That subtext is political. I don't like walls. A wall is fine if its purpose is to protect you and your family so that you don't wake up in the morning to find forest creatures nibbling at your toes. But to me, any wall that does not contain a door and at least one window is more of a prison cell than a form of self-protection. Renga enacts the very meaning of the word, "text," which is from the Latin word "textus," meaning "woven." The goal is to use poetry to weave words, phrases, stanzas, poems, ideas, people, and cultures into a tapestry.

One final note: If you would like to write your own Renga, or even the more open-form Renga variation I use in these poems, I feel the best way to proceed is to listen to as many voices in your imagination as possible, then let your pen guide you down the page, as the voices both converse with and complete one another. All writers, after all, are a bit mad. Novelists imagine plots and poets listen to voices in their heads. But when they do their jobs well, the reader may well feel a little less alone in the world.

Some of the poems in *Renga Variations* first appeared in journals, among them:

"Hotel Breakers,"—*Beltway Poetry, North of Oxford*

"The gift"—*The Beloit Poetry Journal, Another Chicago Magazine, The Xavier Review, Lullwater Review*

"Why I held onto my marbles"—*The Deronda Review, New Mexico Poetry Review, Coal City Review*

I would like to thank Will Wells and Tom Beery for all their help as I wrote these poems. Their advice was very sound and very helpful.

Contents

Renga variation

Gold leaves weaving
their random fates,
scatter philosophy

never learns
what the wind knows

the language
of trees
embracing light

reveals the blue
city is absence,
the lost excluded

middles
have a way
of returning

the darkness, weaving dreams,
binds the scattered stars

cast through the zodiac of fate,
teaching tombstones
to whisper

silence
emptying words,
returns us to touch

the world calling in its winds
to render us whole with wonder.

Light and silence

A honeybee's hum
disturbs the universe
the way

a swallow
touches a celandine
to light and silence

is loss,
is loss trapped in time
dies

when light dies,
and silence listens in the dark

dreams never
realize in words,
cannot preserve time

is light, is light
moving in silence
is memory, is memory

unravels
into time and mystery.

remains always,
knows only
a lost embrace

must be how death feels,
and begins desire

to live
if only as
a cherry's ripening blood

wants what it wants,
wants silence and light,
yet to hear the pulse

of longing is all
the heart needs to begin.

descend
only
when heaven is empty

the mind
to silence,
to light remembering

how all the colors once revealed
more than just their names

only pin the butterfly,
never free it
to light and silence

the darkness that screams,
that refuses to accept
that even loneliness is holy.

Holy the swallow singing silence.
Holy the honeybee engoldening light.

Shasei

started with one stone
glittering in the sun,
limestone sudden silver.

But what to include
concerns us, so much is speaking
and longs to be seen.

Raspberry asterisks
bursting with information…
So much I don't know, life

gone in an instant,
the way clouds spiral into doves
and capture the moon

or this wheat field
reveals the shape of the wind.
Is it hand or harp?

Is it mirror or lamp?
Leads me to hidden lands…
or merely myself?

Each dawn and midnight
translates its private language,
whispering to the reader

Take all the time you need
to record it all in love.

Another music

I seek another music deeper far,
like Orpheus digging for light.

Though for simpler salvations,
this world, I think,
will suffice.

For example,
the intricate cricket's call,
the otherwhere firefly

lonely in August
like a beadsman counting
the stars down to dawn.

or Orpheus now,
the poet as radio
down the far end of the dial.

A voice seeking you
with no seeming author

other than moonlight,
the light of these occasions,
distant frequencies

that guide you from the dead
back to what lives and sings.

Death and magic

I pull a bouquet
of magician's posies
from the deep wound in my side.

The audience laughs and cheers.
They think I'm kidding. I'm not.

I free real doves
from the mess that is my heart,
and send them home to clouds.

I need no assistant.
I throw knives at myself,
missing by inches.

Sawing myself in half
is easy—I'm double now.

Smoke and mirrors—
they mistake my words
for the things they name.

Wait till you see
my disappearing act.
I will die, that's sure.

But by sleight of hand,
they'll think I'm still nearby.

Franz Kline:

"Well look, if I paint what you know, then I will simply bore
you…If I paint what I know, it will be boring to myself.
Therefore, I paint what I don't know"

could fill whole worlds with holes,
or teach ignorance to speak.

Perhaps it's a language
in reverse, a jabberwock
that shows us how not to know.

Perhaps it's a faith,
like the way a cricket call
awaits your response

or silence
softly unfolding the moon

its light
displacing
the darkness

a divine array of not-sure,
an unraveling spool of night

or a meteor—
its message so briefly there,
then erased.

The North Star longing for a prayer,
Venus searching for a door.

I might learn
something
if I learn to paint the wind.

Harold Rosenberg:

"At a certain moment…what was to go on the canvas was not a
picture, but an event"

happens to happen,
earning its own happiness.
Call it voyager

if it needs calling
like love glancing back to you,
wishing to learn your name.

Writing is flying.
The page an ascending angel

or finite eternity, the way
the beetle's intricate clockwork
outlasts the pharaoh's shroud

the way I burn my poems
to send black butterflies to God.

And wind's a wizard,
spiraling gyres into light
that imagines us here

or the way you can
hold a match up to daylight
to guide your longing home.

I see no reason
why a spider weaving suns
is not some kind of redemption.

The way a leaf becomes
an oracle of flight
by accepting its fall.

Jeremy Reed:

"Inner space is a proscribed sanctuary. It is dangerous to go
there"

Yet go we must
to find the electric
underground

hears the dead
speak
the blood we must drink

is memory, is what we've lost,
a detailed picture of the gone

alone,
my father eating
at midnight

my brother's dying
words: "Yes, yes,
thank you, thank you..."

My mother
gluing the night sky
to my bedroom ceiling.

A broken cicada shell
on my grandmother's tombstone.

Go there,
you memory,
make it hurt to beauty.

Concerning

Concerning the rifle you asked about in this photograph where
it's propped against the oak tree while I'm propped there too,
reading Emily Dickinson and looking like I don't want my picture
taken any more than she does:

Because I don't.
It's dangerous inside this frame
It is time frozen dead.

The gun? Well, the gun—
a Winchester '73. Work of art.

No it's not my gun.
I'm a poet, I can't afford
a water pistol

and if I touch it,
I'll probably blow my foot off,
costing my ping-pong scholarship.

But it is a work of art,
like Riefenstahl's nightmare.

It's a metaphor,
and never forget metaphors
can be deadly.

This blue-tinged beauty
might have drilled a perfect hole
through Custer's thick skull

to let some light in,
and life loves light

and though a photograph,
like Custer's fall,
coheres a moment for eternity

It is burrrcold,
cold as a bullet's daydream

Each photograph
marks a death
of something once flowing through time

and below each frame
you should attach this warning:
"Enter at own risk."

The Emerald Tablet:

"As above, so below"

dandelion seed
angels…

I too,
now turning silver,
long for a wind to guide me

and the earth
keeps its ancient patterns
bound to light and soil

a worn-smooth shovel,
its owner
gone to distant fields

I am digging for the moon
in the glaze of the sun

the dragonfly
weaves
a thousand emerald worlds

the oak tree
upside-down,
rooted in the sky.

Is it snowing in heaven too,
this silent, seed-full night?

How to not be you for once

The self is not perfection,
a series of hunches, perhaps,
and a collaboration

created in time,
this who-ness
uncertain of motion

like you are riding backwards on a train
or stepping inside a painting.

Not one heaven
imagined or placed in words
ever seems quite right to me.

This earth feels nearer, its randoming angels
a momentary stay against the night.

T.S. Eliot: "What is Hell? Hell is…oneself. Hell is alone"

Nothing is alone.
The separate is illusion.
We are echoes in mirrors.

Examples:

Deep in the night,
a bullfrog
calling to its mate.

Alligators—
their eyes twin stars.

Fireflies
suturing the night
with gold thread

or dawned spider weaving suns,
wind-blown leaves etching the sky.

We need others.
A lonely ghost
wanders round our bones.

Renga variations—
the many wound round the one.

Boris Pasternak: "You in others — that is your soul"

On fire, the words seek
to light up God's cigar when
he dreamed us into light

when he brought eve to mourning,
divine imperfection in the fall,

splitting the Adam
apple by lovely apple,
bitten into life

by unoriginal sin.
They could not spend eternity
naming all the animals.

They had to grow
beyond the talking snake and garden,
unfolding into love

I first learned joy in another's eyes,
trusting all that silence

our souls bloom breathless
in daring, while neon spiders
weave us into stars.

Two patients in the psyche ward of Mercy Hospital talking to each other in their sleep

Patient One

I fell into a part of me
lonely as a prayer—emptied—
a fugitive of air.

Patient Two

Deeper in lonely than the crow,
your nerves strung like Christmas lights.

Patient One

Yet no one sees you,
and though you are accepted,
you are invisible.

Patient Two

I spoke with winds and weeds once,
but that was long ago.

Patient One

My words I swallowed,
each a world inside a wound
as patient as the moon.

Patient Two

Longing for the moon's secret heart,
hidden on the dark side of time

Patient One

You fear you'll never
escape. They won't let you,
no, not you.

Patient Two

Dreaming of the Holy Vehicle
that leads from self to other.

Patient One

Dreaming we are one,
two halves of the same bright light,
teaching the dark to speak.

John Shoptaw:

"The art of poetry is an art of self-defense"

Like the Sicilian
Dragon daring the white

King prouds over his pawns
while the White Queen watches her chance

is more than a game,
is life and death,
a violence within

to balance violence without,
sensing patterns

knights must move in stealth.
So much depends on the gambit,
open game—risking all

to keep the night at bay,
all that encroaching blood,
that final cornering.

Chess is relation
beyond mere black and white,
beyond mere calculation

each piece is alone
and connected, seeking

the king's temporary victory
over fate, or the knight's
proud bent mane in defeat.

R.H. Blyth:

"The function of the poet is to join what God has divided."

The poet weaves one to many,
rounds many into one.

A new world
upside-down
in the eye of the dragonfly

drawing light within its wings,
and dawn to purple night

apple blossoms
seen briefly in darkness—
Is the moon dreaming them

as it dreams the day to blue
endlessness at noon?

The clear sky,
the clear pond—
which is the mirror?

Basho: "Your poetry issues of its own accord when you and the object have become one."

Yet does this happen before
the poem or during?

Example:

Yeats' dancer
how his words swirl
before and with her dance

Or:

Dear butterfly:
How do you do that,
without getting dizzy?

Its shadow on this sidewalk
erasing its autograph.

Or:

My reflection
in a wet downtown window,
melting into others.

We are alone—then suddenly
a whole world imagines us back.

We are alone—then suddenly
love explodes us into stars.

Basho: "Seeing someone off, his back looks lonely in the autumn wind."

lonely,
the leafswirling wind
within your breath

the way the clothing of the gone
still seems to wear the spirit

of the moon
less round
each night

sheds her faces one by one
to enter eternity.

One grows used to alone,
like two horses
neighing from field to field.

Perhaps the loneliest partings
are meant for beauty alone.

Sute-Jo: "Among the clouds are there also short-cuts? The summer moon."

A cloud,
a child
sings it to light

I have lost, or misplaced
on the dark side of the moon

secret
aliens
dance

a river of stars
guides them
to the child

who dreams them on his ceiling
of phosphorescent constellations.

That child
was me,
gone so far now

only dinosaurs remember,
and only clouds still listen.

Yet sometimes
the aliens still whisper:
"It might be found again."

Look for short-cuts in the clouds.
Look for a doorway in the rain."

Martin Buber: "In the beginning was the relation"

is time and memory
held in a moment

a sudden
quiver
of bird wings

stakes its claim on you,
longs to be seen and heard:

Flower,
incarnation
of light.

Railroad rock ballast
gleaming in the moon.

Bach on the radio,
a spider weaving
with furious joy.

Clarity of hallucination,
a dream that dreams us back.

The poet
corresponding
with every color.

Our greens imagine other worlds.
Our blues go deeper than the stars.

Where is heaven?
The flowers point
in all directions.

Charles Dickens: "Mr. Pickwick thrust his head out of the lattice and looked around him"

And the world looked back,
amazed at its own labyrinth,
minotaur and all.

Streets leading nowhere
or teeming with gold and orphans,

a-swirl with best and worst,
endlessly open to death
of sundry kinds…

Cramped, smothered, gravely-
buried light, as cold as a
bottomless sea…

Mud, fog, ice, disease,
factory, workhouse, prison,
trapdoor, moor, gallows…

bleakening, sweeping, trudging,
starving, combusting, drowning

hunger. The outcast
searching for somewhere
to solve his lonely soul.

Oliver Twist: "Heaven is a long way off"

It's a discipline,
learning to see in the dark,
a cat's precision eye

awaits you here, purr,
and gold molding a world
you never knew could be

a trust, a faith
of walking the darkness,
silk paws, claws of death

moon-sliver your narrowing
eye as you sense the danger

of unknowing,
of going it alone
through another night

search every shadow
to find the one with secrets.
The stars are ghost eyes.

These odd, bent alleys
of your old insomnia
guide your emerald mind.

Your footsteps are notes
in a music score, gone before
others can sing them.

Will you ever find
your pathway to gentle sleep?
A rest from blood and pain?

And does darkness hide all heaven
we may ever know?

Haley Lyndes: "Yes, plants do scream when they're cut—you just can't hear it."

What if they're aware,
all of them—rocks, stones, trees
all woven in pain?

Every atom suffering,
every star wounding the sky

bleeds eternity,
down to the smallest insect,
empty and awake

to its existence,
aloneing in hopeless,
like a twig in deep snow?

It would be too much
to endure without madness,
hearing all those secrets

would blind and deafen
even the relentless Spring
feeling everything

we might have to build a wall
of terrible price, our hearts,
just to enter sleep.

But at cost too great—
our human song.

Gerard Manley Hopkins:

"under the world's splendor and wonder
lies the hidden world
sacred keeping its secrets
hidden from the blind."

And the blind see only what they want to see,
longing only for the known

knows only itself,
feeds full on its own image,
visionless as Pluto.

Yet earth-wise desires
await the patient seeker
knows to dig for stars

inscaping new light
to redream the constellations

and let each world
revolve you whole,
unselving you to other

outrider planets,
rove-over meteors
spun from darkness.

Teachings of the leaves,
all things spell-bent,
imperfect and pure.

All things unseen, unsung,
longing for a voice to find them.

When near is sudden gone

Late November wind—
a single cloud shivers the air

while a forgotten snowman,
covered in ash and sadness,
melts into a tombstone

knows what it knows,
wants what it wants

in, wants deep,
demanding we lose
those we love

are gone now, like an old mad king
whispering strategies

to his taken men,
a mere lone knight
still poised for battle

while a silk-gloved hand
eases the black bishop's
elegant knife

is this star-bled darkness
that longs to reveal
all your deepest fears

and the storm descends, and treetops
are insect crucifixions in the wind.

Hart Crane: "Thou gatherest..."

Gather me, memory,
breathe life to gods and monsters.
and myself to passion and faith.

Raven me back to nightwings
when I spoke the stars awake

not these wounded winds
that send time through every bone,
Novembering my soul

to an endless web
woven from disillusion.

Gather me to graces
free from walls and hate.

Gather me to silent mirrors
that are not ready for regrets.
Bring me back to innocence

that helped me feel the life in things,
and emotion in every color.

Gather me to all your grantings,
Gather me back to love,
imagination reckoning to free.

William Wordsworth: "I wandered lonely as a cloud"

age five, lost but not alone,
I followed a cloud home.

Lost and alone
age five and sixty,
I await the cloud's return.

Like an angel calming near,
or memory come to grace.

This cloud alone
remains the same,
visible in emptiness.

Speaking with the dead

to hear a ghost,
become a ghost

as it empties the house
of your personal
furniture.

Put your eye out.
Poets see best
in half-blindness

And a true wound never closes
but allows the dead to speak.

Death is possible.
He may be thinking
in the next room.

And yet you must not fear,
nor give way to despair.

Even Lycidas
is a ghost story,
haunting the careful reader.

My father's dark room

Master of images.
my father
imagines wounds to light.

The bloody lampshade
his visor

stains the room red,
red air, red air—
the walls sweating blood.

He can photograph absence,
it seems, since I see nothing.

"This is my father,"
he says, a tear falling.
There is no one there.

Tenements, dead streets,
blind windows, skeleton
fire escapes…

He labels each photograph,
but no word meets a mirror.

"Watch the acid there."
The jar beckons, grins,
watching me back.

One by one, his phantoms hang
from the wire, trying to say…

Yet it seems a mere
reflection
in a window long ago

projected into the dark
of a Winter storm.

Muttering,
he baptizes each memory,
hands trembling like frightened birds.

A world I can never enter,
and he can never leave.

The gift

The day my mother
dropped a net of oranges
on the kitchen table

and the oranges rolled and we
snatched them, my brother and I

peeled back the skin
the skin and bit deep to
make the juice explode with our laughter

and my father
spun one orange in his palm
and said quietly: "This was Christmas 1938."

And he said it
without bitterness or anger,
just observing his life from far away,

this tiny world, cupped in one palm.
I learned I had no way
to comprehend an orange.

How to float

"He caaaan't swim,"
said Aunt Edna.
She was right

sank I like a wild duck
diving away from death

taught me to float,
eyes closed,
hands held high

like Superman
without superpowers,

except to float
and float, without end,
letting the waves wonder

me where they will,
unfathomed to all the lifeguards

never saw
what I saw
deep on the ocean floor

creatures like spun glass,
blue and green and gold—

eyes that watched
me with
the patience of stars

looking back
at me refusing
to fly or drown

I learned to float like silence
moving from word to word.

Hotel Breakers

The sea, the sea is breaking up—
Oh mother, where are the sails?

Shh, darling, shh…
tides come in, tides go out,
our sleep is their song.

I cannot sleep…
the moon, oh my sweet mother,
Grandfather's dying face…

Sleep, my love, just sleep…
Listen to the silence dreaming…

Mother, a moonlit skeleton
is dancing on the waves!

It cannot hurt us
here, my child,
it dances all alone.

She soothes my cheek with gentle hand,
and whispers in my ear:

The sands go shh, shh, shhh…
The stars weave us, love,
into their net of dreams…

And the sea is both our voices now,
my son, it sets us free.

The diamond was a fool

The diamond was a fool,
four bases and a rulebook,
a self-enclosed world.

This metal clothesline pole
was second base, small tree first,
third a shed.

This is not for nostalgia,
that sentimental cruelty.

The players are dead—
two from war, two from disease,
one from suicide.

I and this pole the sole survivors,
everything else—gone.

Even the houses
no longer know each other,
the trees tall and strong.

I search the air for clues.
They're here—in the falling leaves
blown back into questions.

I surrender to these winds.
Loss has no tongue to tell it.

Joso:

"Colder even than the snow,
the Winter moon
on white hairs"

is how time must travel,
appalling the body

mind and blood
and misplacing words
once safe at home

Even home now a mystery,
leaving us clues to the gone.

My father's glasses
found in an old drawer,
stare at me in wonder.

How will he see in the other world?
Or read words he left behind?

A gnawed old pen—
even our teeth marks
survive us.

His suits hang alone,
keeping his Rexall After-Shave scent

The past is empty but
to touch, smell, or sounds
between silences.

My mother's song
still haunting
her swing.

A fence in a snowfield
divides nothing from itself.

We inherit
only the blank page,
a sliver of the moon.

Pierre Reverdy:

"The wind circles. A cry is heard…The lamp has just gone out."

Memory lamp
clinging
to darkness

whose stubborn ghosts
possess the furniture

the walls
the past
waits within.

A wind here is a hand,
trying to pluck my bones.

Poe(try)
digs
beneath floorboards

somewhere
might be joy
purged of night

mares, or at least of children
weeping blood and hunger.

The depths beneath
the basement
whisper a buried life.

Memory,
ripe as a root cellar, bursts.

Jack Spicer: "You are dead and the dead are very patient"

ghosts
awaiting transmission

the way a crow flies
tracing the path
where the dark lives

outcast in sunlight,
wounded by neglect

the poet of night
voices
starving in a public park

or angel
beneath the crawlspace
writing her body to God

the infecting word
dreaming of the rose

the way your own falling
binds you to the stars

undream
the real
to speak the dead

dive to the bottom,
no mere Orizaba
denies the poet

his eternal grail of laughter,
his spindrift watching God

the dream song sings
from the bridge
forgiving the fall.

Jack Spicer: "Between two silences"

are conversations
linking both sides of a wall,
ignoring imposition

words rising to free,
randoming as fireflies,
aimed toward the future perfect,

a performance of the real,
a doorway in the rain

entered, yes, yes, by
lovers, whose passion cries
fill the world with longing

to be in grass and
flesh and breath and bone, dreaming

folds and unfolds
like your grandmother's memories
opening into love

poems or light
to embrace the possible
from breath to breath

together they speak the new—
Together they enter into life.

Issa:

"Crescent moon
bent to the shape
of the cold"

brings the moon inside our breaths,
brings the night inside our blood.

An abacus of worlds
spinning
round their fates

those ascending
skeletons of stars

"are whispering to each other."
What heart are we
not to listen to the light?

Or how learn ourselves
without this darkness blessing?

The poem
a gentle conversation
drifting ghost to ghost.

Father and son

Issa:

"A world of dew
is the world of dew,
and yet, and yet…"

the lost return
in visions of the fathers
stepping through the doors of memory

dreams only of return,
a mere moment

to be held, fully held
if only for a last time,
in the sunrisen grass.

To want, to love

I want everything
I can embrace

a wound
that learns
to heal itself

or if not, then healed by another
self, also bearing wounds.

I want to learn why
I was once my mother's joy,
when my heart traced suns.

I want to be haunted
by ghosts of divinity.

I want the angels returned
to my grandmother's
laundry line of winds.

I want my marbles back,
so I may roll them to other worlds.

I want
the heart of light,
the Absolute Rose.

But if this be a vain dream,
love, teach me to write in mid-air,
like the butterfly.

Memory

Viridian
nightmirror
longing for dawn

I rest on a hill in the mirror,
watching sapphire worlds unwind
and a fading moon
alone in breathless mists

the grass shimmers alive,
the sky
a blue within the blue

diamonds
sparkling in the trees

and green dinosaurs
without tooth or claw,
graze lazily around

my book of wizards and pirates
for a pillow.

The mirror
shatters,
wounding time

and I float from my bedroom window,
learn all life is geometric

line, square, circles of shadow,
the string my mother ties round my wrist
to keep me from floating to stars.

The townfolk don't believe me
but whenever I return

I show them pictures
from my night journeys,
images from their hidden lives.

Frank O'Hara: "Grace to be born and live as variously as possible"

moments arounding you
to a breathless here

reflecting heaven
in the glint of sunlight
on wet stones

"and always embrace things,
people, earth, sky, stars,
as I do."

while the world
unfolds itself
like an answered question

or intricate crickets
design the darkness

reveals
the firefly,
here-there-here-there

He advertises himself.
He's open all night.

Frank O'Hara: "Space becomes a field of incident"

to float the self
like a leaf on a clear pond,
tracing the clouds

watch the leaf nearing,
its song for you, your dream
of falling to God.

Now you are master
of geography! The world
your map of wonders.

And more—coloratura
of spheres unwinding time.

Look…
You see, hear, touch
all things to free.

And each thing you find
both hides and reveals itself.

Holiness is near,
a snail that crawls through the soul
binds you in time and love.

Frank O'Hara: "The gentle are curious, but the curious are not gentle"

and unwhole themselves,
they want you clearly defined.

You are built all wrong,
they say, but who taught them
anatomy?

Who carved that letter
H on your chest,
then sat back in horror?

Who first slammed you
into the corner-pocket?
Who took your game away?

Who denied your hands are wings
meant to brush the stars?

Who cast you where alleys
speak to the fire escapes,
and closets talk to themselves?

You are a message
locked in a bottle,
floating on silent seas.

Come. Speak. Touch. Until
the clouds take you to better worlds.

Frank O'Hara: "Now please tell me...If the surface isn't kept up"

Sometimes the surface is enough
to enter the world with a breath

like a fragile dance
between two glass lovers
turning in the moonlight

let the poem free
where the wind wants to take it.
Let possibles come

in a glance of wings
unfolding the dawn
guess another world

the way carousel horses
frozen in late autumn
await the springing sun.

To the Sybil of Cumae

Prophesy leaves
breaking
into light.

Longing to die, each leaf
sends itself to eternity

syllables
just this side
of revelation.

Like a black cat at sundown,
you move between two worlds.

Like you,
I am old,
and must endure.

Your life
is one long cruelty,
your death immortal.

I am a mere reader,
the one who records
silence and love.

Watch time break in my hands,
and scatter itself in memories.

Frank O'Hara:

"The frail
instant
needs us"

But not to tell us what to do,
or point some fated destiny…

I don't like teleology,
since I never know
where I'm going

and everything
about eschatology
scares the hell out of me.

Let's have a world free
of teleoes eschas.

Myth
is cruelty
embodied

chaos
disguised as order

or ancient blood
pretending
to be reborn

an old man
whistling like wind through a skull

fate hobbled off-scene
with Oedipus
and his third leg.

Never sleep with a woman
old enough to be your mother

or kill anyone
old enough
to be your father.

How difficult is that?
Let's kill no one today.

The war gods
long
for our death.

I'd rather translate bullfrog,
or teach a star how to sing.

John Ashbery: "In words broken open and pressed to the mouth"

comes the holy silence
as it breaks from heaven free

sentences to stanza
rooms with opening doors
and wiggly walls

with holes too wide for fingers,
with windows wide as joy

to include the whole world
in a single breath, if breath
be silent as a prayer

to break the mind free,
and wonder the heart to love.

John Ashbery: "The pleasure that you get if you love poetry, is a pleasure that's going to cause you to act, it forces you back into life"

or forward into flowing living,
a breathless joy in motion...

the impermanent
precision of a snowflake
alone in tumbling

I am othering
again, imaging myself
invisible into

this Winter crowd
has no center, questions
each fragile moment

is Christmasing
silver bells dispelling time,
and I am nowhere

here, adrift in angel breaths
of all these many and alone

I love, I wide open,
casting myself to winds
weaving my words to sound.

I am the motion of souls
dreaming this world alive

unquestioning I
unravel into light,
just to be and be

with no bright star of fate
to guide the three fools in,
muttering crucifixions.

I'm more like a fly,
his eyes two blue Christmas bulbs
reflecting heaven

upside-down
in sixteen simultaneous
incarnations.

William Wordsworth: "Imagination...a plastic power"

Imagination
flowing line to line

room to room,
the stanza
with a hole in it,

sun to moon
rhythm and the sea

systole to diastole,
human
to divine

takes a while, be patient,
or it could come all at once...

Wait until
the poem
speaks itself

like lighting one candle with another,
teaching darkness to listen.

word
flesh
page

your blood all the ink you'll need
Bite your wrist to drink the dreaming there.

Unravel the known
to reveal the fire
in things.

William Wordsworth: "To hold fit converse with the spiritual world"

comes at the price of silence,
hidden behind eternity.

No tearful vigil,
but grin-secret joy,
alive in nowhere.

I lived by hiding,
learning to speak to silence,
forgetting myself.

Alone and away from armies,
Alone, alive, untouched!

OhIcouldhideanywhere as a child, inside a closet, thumbed in a
thimble, clasped in a book, spun in a wind-thinking leaf, a
memory, a bug, a lonely planet searching for moons, inside my
head, under the bed, inside the bed disguised as tossed blankets,
in the silence between snowmen, the window-seat was best of
all, I disappeared watching the birds land on the windowsill for
sunflowers in their beautiful trust of the invisible…

Solitary confinement!
I chose it to set me free.

And when I was born.
I stepped through the window
and a tearful garden

welcomed me in a
jeweled embrace. I fell and fell
through a painful green,

cut by a thousand stars,
I was the snake's bright stare,
all hiss and knowing.

I wounded the air
with my breaths and cries, I bled
down every tree,

my nerves strung branch to branch,
shivering down every leaf.

Now my flesh is written
through the grass. Come read me here,
and find another world.

Li Po: I sit and plumb whole kalpas, see through heaven and earth empty."

Empty?
Well, still
it glitters illusions

like a movie set, whole towns
mere cardboard or hologram

the City Bank,
my hand passes
right through

the whole scene
scripted
elsewhere

suddenly is here, hidden
universe, just behind ours

like the silence
between
drops of rain

yet empty, yes, I'll grant you,
like a blue sky is empty of stars

or a cicada shell
empties itself
for flight

or light to color,
color
to night.

All things speak what they are not,
like nohow and contrariwise.

The Red King
dreaming
of the mirror.

Li Po: "Words of the Immortals, Bones of the Tao"

Banished Immortals—our mountains
no longer reach to the gods

have left the earth
abandoned to longing,
yet ripe for wars.

I've seen one banished immortal
living all alone on the moon.

Moonflower
heaven's
incarnation,

sometimes he descends to earth,
playing his flute in shadows,

sings "Men have lost
the holy night
within."

Only he sings this song,
walking from silence to silence

feeding on darkness,
drinking from a cup
of light,

watching the moon's
phases of emptiness.

In the Sea of Tranquility
he writes
with a pen filled with loss and wine.

On the day of another mass shooting

A ladybug
inching up my telescope
aiming at the moon.

A sparrow nesting
behind
the movie marquee.

Pigeons
returning
to the burned-down church.

A young girl
writing her name
on a wet window.

Without such illuminations,
I don't think I could live.

W.B. Yeats: "We have fed the heart on fanta-sies/The heart's grown brutal from the fare"

From fare we consumed,
we conjured a dream
of a riverboat con-man

smooth as an antique doorknob
drawing cards to trumps.

Watch as he pockets
contradictory cards,
then hands them out like souls.

His seems could be anything—
kaleidoscope chameleon,

surface to surface,
a series of pasteboard masks
or absence visible.

and being nothing himself,
capable of anything.

He walls and walls and walls
an innocence that never was,
a city on a crumbling hill.

Normals a nightmare
shimmering from his bones,
releasing ghosts…

In the end we get
the apocalypse we dreamed
goes round, comes home again.

John Berryman: "Yet some *have* escaped…We ask God…to take the walls away."

and this gentles us,
frees us from glooming doom,
opens light within

escapes us into others
who share our lonely song

TEAR DOWN ALL THE WALLS,
our need for them long gone.

It was fear built them
from blocks of heartless stone,
wary of the dark within.

Pain is all they brought,
terror of all alone,

Good neighbors,
unplunge the fence posts.
True gods go deeper far.

Paul Celan: "There are still songs to sing beyond mankind"

where silence reigns,
one finger to its lips.

A death index, names
stacked in ordered columns.

Impeccable research,
pure historical method
weaving madness.

Names, names, effaced in snow,
bleeding ink and numbers.

How to read them now?
What do graves say?
"Silence speaks the language of stones."

Paul Celan: "Poetry breathes you in"

to the breathcrystal
rootsyllable of the lost

other bound in time
and silence

waiting here,
streaks in the eyes,
blood in the snow

the word without echo
from eternity

a mother's cry
not yet forgotten.
And so we hold on…

The poem resays the world,
weaving the past a voice.

Paul Celan: "Go with art into your own corner. And set yourself free"

to re-member
what hate tore
asunder

a son redeemed, re-dreamed
into a broken heartword

his people, ours,
trapped in an hourglass
sand-memory, rain of sand

sent to the death-stanza
await in darkness
tongues of barbed wire.

a freeing, an opening,
a meridian listens for the lost.

Yegor Chegrinets: "You cannot escape the war here. It just grows out of the earth"

comes time ticking blood
in words that cannot redeem

the dead cannot speak
though they sprout here
bone by bone by bone

alone, unredeemed,
wary of rebirth.

Prayer

In this fallen world,
where spiders crawl up the moon,
glow my faith to life.

Aware me to an inkling
of what my love bestows

And though cruel blackbirds
swirl like furious bibles,
teach me to be kind.

Fugitive my hates
that kept me from my song.

Let imagination,
that seeks another's touch,
light like fireflies

so unexpected, sudden grace,
an old man's heart embrace

Eugenio Montale: "See, in these silences where things give over and seem on the verge of betraying their final secret"

silence is a wound,
"mutilate"—
Montale's word for

"wounded" is closer,
mutilated, like wingless
birds dreaming of the

sun, watching the sky
for secrets of flight
or a last betrayal.

What, after all,
is this mystery of wings
but love of other worlds?

This verging of things,
revelation always hiding
round the next nearing cloud.

Words come wounded from the moon,
our lone response to silence,
whispers in the night.

Rilke: "I can open to another life that's wide and timeless"

clouds and winds
folding into one

invisible
cicadas
sing the tree electric

while electric underground
traces darkness bone by bone

irradiating
arterial roots
that feed on the past

opens to the stars
astray unwinding
time to eternity

and opens to the day,
cloud-shadow light-swarms
learning to speak the earth.

Just dance. You will do.
Now enter the world.

Why I held onto my marbles

Because they were
religious, useless,
fragile and fearless.

Because they circled the world,
and took the form of my Summer dreams.

Because whoever
invented marbles
must have thought angels were round.

Because
the chipped ones
were more beautiful.

Because the distance of their journeys
was an exact equation of space and time.

Because
there were rules,
and this calmed me full.

Because they were earth, sun, moon and stars
cupped in the palm of one hand.

Because they spun the sun
into diamonds, and sparkled
like snake eyes in the moon.

Because when they surrounded me,
I was safe from armies of sadness.

Because a pretty girl
once blew on my cat's eye
and made it glow.

Because a purie contains emotions
it took me thirty years to comprehend.

Because when I found them again,
in my aging parents' basement,
buried under old Christmases,
and half a life of loss
and illusion,
they remembered.

How to ride your bicycle with no hands

Eyes closed, hands on chrome,
breath in timing with the wheels,
mind a gyroscope.

Trust the wind, the wheels,
the chrome, the pedals, your breath,
whatever needs trusting.

Now let your hands—go.
You're alive in the pink light
under your eyelids!

You will realize
with a laugh that sets you free
there is nothing to fear.

No need for light, wind, chrome,
pedals, wheels or gyroscope.
You can't fall off the earth.

Bob Kaufman: "Drinking cool Beatitudes"

while sea clouds turn to doves
and capture the moon.

A spider weaves her web with suns,
threading her darkest dreams.

And when the sun sets,
stars conspire, and shadows
wander in search of souls.

What isn't a vision?

Li Po: "You can reach out and touch the stars"

I borrow a few,
place them gently
in my pocket.

Soon I'm a whole universe,
and all my words come out in light

is darkness
finally
learning to see

Why fear my last days?
Why count the nights of dread
or quarrel with time?

this dream world of day and night
is only a dream world after all.

Prospero: "This insubstantial fabric"

conversations with the dead…
I can't really talk to you.
You seem content with darkness.

Yet sometimes you change with memory,
or wander world to world.

You never weep there, do you?
You've no living blood
to dance, your books closed.

And you won't give up your secrets
to any mortal word.

So I leave you now
to face the living silence,
that hides on the edge of things.

A conversation
depends on two absurdities
learning to love.

Last vesper

A true wound never heals.
It merely craves a meaning.
I climb the tree you blessed me long ago

to find the joy I once knew,
alone in all your greening

Time has willed me memories.
Some cut deep with every graven word.
Some glimmer with secret planets.

You grant me these arms to embrace you,
a leaf-whispered grace, moon circles above.

I your shy singer in this chasuble,
since the sun grew weary of its gods
I trace our heartbeats root to stars

every lost tree in this forest you are here
and distant as the shadow of a gull.

The firefly memory

I chase a firefly
so long ago
only the wind remembers.

I stop, it stops, I advance,
it recedes, deep in the wheat.

Its glow could pulse a ring,
though its joy be Easter size,
awaits me near and far.

Wanders—here—there—a distant
lighthouse floating in the mist.

It wonders me lost
and found, this key to secret
worlds, doorless and free.

And now it hundreds itself
like scattered gold or watching eyes.

And I go with them
so briefly hint at heaven
trying for the moon.

Dawn, they fade in silent harmony,
seeking the stars that dreamed them into light.

The fallen unfallen tree

Can it see, or feel
its reflection in the night river
beckoning from below?

Birds will not alight it, clouds
pass by in blind unknowing.

Its roots still embrace
all the fire in things,
branches cold and bare.

Above-ground gnarled arteries
counting stars and cricket pulses.

Does it long for earth,
life's dark remainder?
Or eternal flow of light?

It leans overlooking its fate,
loving both at once.